Organic Farming

Dona Herweck Rice

Smithsonian

Contributing Author

Heather Schultz, M.A.

Consultants

Cindy Brown
Supervisory Horticulturalist Collections Specialist
Smithsonian Gardens

Tamieka Grizzle, Ed.D.
K–5 STEM Lab Instructor
Harmony Leland Elementary School

Stephanie Anastasopoulos, M.Ed.
TOSA, STREAM Integration
Solana Beach School District

Publishing Credits

Rachelle Cracchiolo, M.S.Ed., *Publisher*
Conni Medina, M.A.Ed., *Managing Editor*
Diana Kenney, M.A.Ed., NBCT, *Series Developer*
June Kikuchi, *Content Director*
Véronique Bos, *Creative Director*
Robin Erickson, *Art Director*
Seth Rogers, *Editor*
Mindy Duits, *Senior Graphic Designer*
Smithsonian Science Education Center

Image Credits: p.6 National Geographic Creative/Alamy; p.8 (all) © Smithsonian; p.9 (right) Vladimir Zhoga/Shutterstock; p.14 (top) Fox Photos/Getty Images; p.15 Denver Post via Getty Images; p.18 Georg Gerster/Science Source; p.19 (bottom) Jim West/Science Source; p.20 (left) Dennis Kunkel Microscopy/Science Source; pp.22–23 Konrad Wothe/Minden Pictures; p.23 (top) Aaron Burden; p.25 (bottom) Scott Linstead/Science Source; all other images iStock and/or Shutterstock.

Library of Congress Cataloging-in-Publication Data

Names: Rice, Dona, author.
Title: Organic farming / Dona Herweck Rice.
Description: Huntington Beach, CA : Teacher Created Materials, 2018. |
Includes index. |
Identifiers: LCCN 2018005208 (print) | LCCN 2018007093 (ebook) | ISBN
9781493869329 (E-book) | ISBN 9781493866922 (pbk.)
Subjects: LCSH: Organic farming--Juvenile literature.
Classification: LCC S605.5 (ebook) | LCC S605.5 .R525 2018 (print) | DDC
631.5/84--dc23
LC record available at https://lccn.loc.gov/2018005208

Smithsonian

Teacher Created Materials

5301 Oceanus Drive
Huntington Beach, CA 92649-1030
www.tcmpub.com

ISBN 978-1-4938-6692-2

Table of Contents

Food, Glorious Food!

There are few things in life that everyone thinks about every day. Food is one of them. Throughout the day, a person often thinks: *What is there to eat? I wonder what we're having for dinner. My stomach is growling. Oh, that smells good! I'm hungry!*

Food is necessary for life, but it can also be one of life's pleasures. People like food that tastes good! More than anything, though, healthy bodies need **nutritious** food. Unfortunately, a lot of foods that people eat are not nutritious. They may taste good and provide fuel for the body, but they are not nourishing. Sometimes, they are downright unhealthy.

Over time, a growing number of people have chosen more healthy food choices. They want food to be delicious *and* nutritious.

A woman works with lettuce in a garden.

About 1 in 10 workers in the United States works in the food industry.

Preparing healthy foods can be fun!

Back to the Roots

Foods we think are healthy may be made or grown in unhealthy ways. More and more people are worried about this fact. So, researchers studied how people farm today. They compared current methods to how people used to farm. Today's **organic** farmers are going back to the roots of farming.

History of Farming

Farming is one of the biggest industries in the world. But people have not always farmed. In ancient times, people found food by **foraging**. These people were called hunter-gatherers. Then, thousands of years ago, people began to farm.

Farming did not start in just one place with one group of people. Several groups began to farm around the same time. The first farmers lived throughout the so-called **Fertile** Crescent. It is a large area of land in the Middle East. It has rich soil and plenty of water.

This drawing shows farmers planting seeds in the Fertile Crescent.

SCIENCE

Fertile Crescent

Plants need soil that is rich with **nutrients**. The soil in the Fertile Crescent has nutrients that are needed for a variety of plants to grow. **Sediment** from the flowing rivers fertilizes the soil. The climate is right for year-round growing cycles. An abundant water supply brings needed water to crops.

Most early farming was done by hand. People buried seeds in soil, pulled weeds, and **harvested** plants without machines.

As time went on, people developed basic farming tools. They used sticks and bones to dig into soil. When they learned to work with metal, people made hoes, scythes (SIGHTHS), and plows. These tools could do more than hands could. People also used animals to help them farm.

Farming continued this way for thousands of years. Most people farmed or lived near farms and grew crops for their families and communities. Nature nourished and watered plants. Farmers worked with nature to grow the plants just as they would grow naturally. They learned to work with natural processes to grow healthy plants that would, in turn, keep them healthy, too.

prehistoric hoe

modern hoe with a metal blade

TECHNOLOGY

Which Tool to Use?

Machetes (muh-SHEH-teez) and scythes have long been used to harvest crops. The size, weight, and structure of each tool make them easier to swing at a certain height. A machete is a wide and sturdy blade with a short handle. It is best used to harvest crops that grow waist high. A scythe is a hooked blade attached to a long wooden pole. It is best for cutting crops close to the ground.

The Gifts of Farming

Farming became a valuable practice for many reasons. It produced an ongoing food supply. People did not have to search for food or follow animal herds. They could grow food and store what they needed. With farming, they were much more likely to have the food they needed year-round.

Farming also helped people stay in one place. They could build homes and communities. They could also raise farm animals such as goats, sheep, and pigs. These animals were food sources as well.

Having a steady supply of food also gave people time. With time, they could make their lives better. They became inventors and scientists. When people do not have to struggle for their basic needs, they have the chance to grow in many ways.

A farmer uses a tractor to pull a plow.

This woodcut shows early farmers in a barn with cows.

A $\frac{1}{2}$ kilogram (1 pound) of wool can be spun to make about $1\frac{1}{2}$ kilometers (1 mile) of yarn! One sheep can grow up to 14 kg (30 lb.) of wool each year.

Natural Food Revolution

Farming methods did not change for thousands of years. Then, new inventions started to change how people farmed. The Industrial Revolution took place in the 1800s. It began in England and spread through much of the world. It was a time when people found ways to make more goods. Machines, such as the wheat thresher, were built to help farmers harvest food faster. More people worked in cities, and fewer people farmed. More food than ever before was needed to feed all the people. Food was shipped across countries and around the world.

To meet the demand for food, chemicals were used to get rid of pests and to help plants grow faster. More and more animals were raised for food. They were often treated poorly. Fats, sugars, and chemicals were added to foods. These things made food taste better. Food became less natural and more **manufactured**.

In many places, people started to gain weight. Foods high in fat and sugar affected people's health. Some people began to notice. They wanted to see a change. They wanted to get back to nature and nature-made food.

caged chickens

free-range chickens

wheat thresher

ENGINEERING

Harvesting

Harvesting fruits and nuts from trees can be tricky. The food must be removed without hurting trees or the food. To solve some of these problems, people have made clever inventions. A device called a harvester was invented that shakes certain nut trees so the nuts fall. Trees are not harmed, and nuts can be gathered from the ground.

Going Natural

Big changes took place in the 1960s and 1970s. People questioned how things were done. One of those things was growing food. Many people wanted to go back to the old ways of doing things. They wanted to become more natural. They did not work in traditional jobs. They told people to think for themselves instead of following other people's rules. They thought **mass-produced** food was unhealthy. They also thought the way that some food was made was bad for the environment. Many people thought it was cruel to eat animals. These people wanted change.

Workers in a factory fill cans with beans.

Vegetarian diets became popular. People opened restaurants that did not serve meat. Some people joined together to create food co-ops. Co-ops are groups in which people share the food they grow or make with the rest of the group. In this way, there was plenty of healthy food for everyone.

vegetarian foods

A woman works at a vegetarian booth at the 1979 Capitol Hill People's Fair.

Organic Farming Must-Haves

Growing food naturally means farmers need to change how they work. Instead of using man-made fertilizers, organic farmers choose to use natural methods. Crops grown this way do not grow as large or as fast as crops grown with synthetic fertilizers. But soil stays healthy over time. Synthetic fertilizer helps plants grow quickly but does not usually help the soil.

To keep soil healthy with natural methods, farmers need a few things. The first thing they need is patience!

Patience

Organic farming takes time and care. There are no shortcuts. Farmers must work to keep the soil healthy. Plants must be allowed to grow naturally, without chemicals. A lot of farm work must be done by hand. Farm animals need space to roam. Farmers must care for them humanely as well. Farmers must also rotate their crops and use compost—a mixture of dead plants. All of this takes patience.

A farmer stands in a wheat field.

Sprouts push through healthy soil.

Organic farming does not mean chemical-free farming. Over 20 chemicals have been approved by U.S. Organic Standards and are used in the growing of organic crops.

Crop Rotation

Crop rotation is the process in which farmers change the crops they grow in their fields in a special order. For example, if a farmer has three fields, he or she may grow carrots in the first field, green beans in the second, and tomatoes in the third. The next year, green beans will be in the first field, tomatoes in the second field, and carrots will be in the third. Year three, the crops will rotate again. By the fourth year, the crops will go back to their original order. Each crop nourishes the soil for the next crop. This type of farming is **sustainable** because the soil stays healthy.

When the same type of crop is planted in a field again and again, it uses all the nutrients in the soil. Pests and diseases that are common to that crop increase. This type of farming is not sustainable. Soil may become barren. In barren soil, crops have trouble growing or do not grow at all.

crop rotation

Two students plant onions in a hoop house.

ARTS

Hoop Houses

The U.S. Department of **Agriculture** offers plans for organic farming. Hoop house plans, that is! Hoop houses capture solar energy. The hoop design extends the growing season far beyond summer. With hoops, fresh harvests can happen deep into winter!

Compost

Compost is fertilizer that nature makes. Plants **decompose** in nature. Their nutrients return to the soil. Then, they nourish new plants.

Farmers make compost with layers of dead plant matter. Stirring the layers helps make good fertilizer. Compost can be spread among rows of plants and mixed into soil. It keeps soil healthy. Healthy soil means healthy plants.

The **microorganisms** in soil and compost do a lot of work. These tiny life forms are always busy! They break down plant matter. They **aerate** soil. Without them, plants would not grow. Microorganisms in soil are also **diverse**. In fact, they are more diverse than living things in any other ecosystem. This variety is important. It helps create a healthy balance in an ecosystem. With diversity, every living thing gets what it needs. Compost helps keep the diversity in soil strong.

microorganisms

soil compost

This illustration shows worms aerating soil.

Worms are often used to make compost. They make tunnels for air and water as they move through soil.

Going Buggy

Every healthy ecosystem includes a variety of living things. These things need each other to survive and thrive. It is true that there are many insects that can harm plants. But there are other insects that plants need to grow well. To help their crops, farmers can grow certain plants to attract those useful insects. A portion of a healthy organic farm should be set aside to attract these insects.

Helpful insects can be grouped into three main categories. The first category is pollinators. The second is predators. And the third is parasites. Each group has its own place in an organic farm.

Pollinators

Pollinators are essential to plant life. They spread pollen. Pollen helps plants make seeds. In turn, the plants provide food for the insects. They help one another.

One of the most important pollinators is the honeybee. Without bees, much of the plant life on Earth would die out. Bees are really that important!

a bee covered in pollen

A honeybee collects pollen from a flower.

MATHEMATICS

Balance of Nutrients

Plants need nutrients to grow. Organic farmers can test soil to measure the levels of nutrients. Then, they can add just what the crop needs. If there is too little of any nutrient, compost and soil additives can make it right.

Predators

Insect predators are like any other predator. They kill prey. These helpful insects can be quite useful against pests. They might even be an organic farmer's best friends!

In farming, the ladybug is an important predator. This colorful beetle can rid crops of aphids. Aphids suck fluids from plants. This can kill plants. Ladybugs eat aphids. A ladybug might kill thousands of aphids throughout its lifetime. No wonder many people think of ladybugs as good luck!

Parasites

Parasites use insect pests to feed their young. The young live off the captured pests. Parasites even store pests to feed their offspring as they grow.

For example, parasitic wasps eat bugs that are harmful to crops. These wasps do a great service to farmers.

With just the right helpful bugs, a farmer can avoid using chemicals to kill pests. Pests are controlled naturally.

Wasp larvae feed on a bug.

A wasp collects food for its young.

A ladybug eats an aphid.

Ladybugs can be kept **dormant** for a few weeks in a refrigerator! This way, they can be stored and used when they are needed in a garden.

Food for Thought

There is no getting around the fact that all living and nonliving things are connected. Each thing on Earth can affect everything else—and can be affected, too. What is in the air affects those who breathe it. What is in the water affects those who drink it. What is in the soil affects food that grows in it. And what is in each plant and animal affects those who eat them.

Perhaps it makes sense, then, for things to be grown naturally. Farmers have been growing plants organically for thousands of years and the plants are thriving. Today, people are farming by hand and keeping the soil healthy by rotating crops. It may seem hard, but you can grow organically, too. That way, you can be sure you are eating the best food possible. Organic farming keeps plants, animals, and soil healthy. But it keeps people healthy, too. So, go plant some fruits and vegetables, and remember—go organic!

Organic farming may be natural, but it is not cheap! These foods can cost much more than mass-produced foods.

STEAM CHALLENGE

Define the Problem

Your school's garden club is having trouble growing organic crops in the winter. They are asking students to present possible solutions. Create a model structure that will provide safe growing conditions for crops during the winter.

Constraints: The length, width, and height of your model must be between 0.75 and 1 meter (2.5 and 3 feet).

Criteria: The protective structure must allow sunlight in, include an entryway, and withstand a 30-second wind test.

1 Research and Brainstorm

What are the crops' basic needs? How will your structure meet these needs? How can you make your structure stable?

2 Design and Build

Sketch your design. What materials will work best? What purpose will each part serve? Build the model.

3 Test and Improve

Present your model to your classmates to evaluate the first two criteria. Use a large fan to conduct a 30 second wind test. Get feedback. Does your model meet all of the criteria? How can you improve it? Modify your design and try again.

4 Reflect and Share

How can you make your structure visually appealing? Will your model produce crops in all weather conditions?

Glossary

aerate—to add air or gas to something

agriculture—the science or occupation of farming

decompose—to be slowly broken down and destroyed by natural processes

diverse—varied, or different from each other

dormant—not active but able to become active

fertile—able to reproduce or to support reproduction

foraging—searching for food

harvested—gathered or took in

humanely—done with kindness and respect

manufactured—produced in large amounts using machinery

mass-produced—made in large amounts

microorganisms—tiny living things that can be seen only by using a microscope

nutrients—substances that living things need for life

nutritious—providing what is needed for health and growth

organic—grown or made naturally

sediment—material (such as stones, clay, and sand) that settles to the bottom of a liquid

sustainable—made to continue to exist; easily maintained

synthetic—something made by combining different man-made substances

toxins—organic poisons

vegetarian—not containing meat

Index

CAREER ADVICE
from Smithsonian

Do you want to run a farm?
Here are some tips to get you started.

"Victory Gardens were planted during World War I and II to help feed the people. There is a Victory Garden at the National Museum of American History. It's a place where people can talk about and learn how to grow organic food. Research the kinds of fruits and vegetables that grow well where you live. Then, try planting some of them. You will learn how to keep crops healthy. Plus, you can grab a healthy snack whenever you want one!"—***Susan Evans, Food History Program Director***

"Running a successful farm is like being the president of a business. You need to learn about finances and marketing. You also need to learn about weather, Earth science, chemistry, and biology."—***Cindy Brown, Supervisory Horticulturalist Collections Specialist***